Unofficial GUIDES JUNIOR

Fortnite's Island

By Josh Gregory

Metropolitan Library System

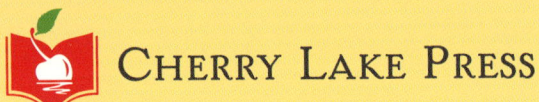

Published in the United States of America by
Cherry Lake Publishing
Ann Arbor, Michigan
www.cherrylakepublishing.com

Reading Adviser: Marla Conn MS, Ed., Literacy specialist, Read-Ability, Inc.

Copyright ©2021 by Cherry Lake Publishing
All rights reserved. No part of this book may be reproduced or utilized in any form or by any means without written permission from the publisher.

Library of Congress Cataloging-in-Publication Data

Names: Gregory, Josh, author.
Title: Fortnite's island / by Josh Gregory.
Description: Ann Arbor, Michigan : Cherry Lake Publishing, 2020. | Series: Unofficial guides junior | Includes bibliographical references and index. | Audience: Grades 2-3 | Summary: "With more than 250 million players around the world, Fortnite is one of the most popular video games in history. In this book, readers will tour the vast and varied island where the game's matches take place. Includes table of contents, author biography, sidebars, glossary, index, and informative backmatter"— Provided by publisher.
Identifiers: LCCN 2020010168 | ISBN 9781534169630 (library binding) | ISBN 9781534171312 (paperback) | ISBN 9781534173156 (pdf) | ISBN 9781534174993 (ebook)
Subjects: LCSH: Fortnite Battle Royale (Game)—Juvenile literature.
Classification: LCC GV1469.35.F67 G7487 2020 | DDC 794.8—dc23
LC record available at https://lccn.loc.gov/2020010168

Cherry Lake Publishing would like to acknowledge the work of the Partnership for 21st Century Learning, a Network of Battelle for Kids. Please visit *http://www.battelleforkids.org/networks/p21* for more information.

Printed in the United States of America
Corporate Graphics

Table of Contents

One Big World 5

Plenty to See 7

Learning Your Way Around 9

Checking the Map 11

Deciding Where to Drop 13

Filling in the Blanks 15

Seeking Out Supplies 17

A Faster Way to Travel 19

Gaining an Advantage 21

Glossary 22

Find Out More 23

Index 24

About the Author 24

Fortnite's world is way too big to see everything in a single match.

One Big World

There's no other game quite like *Fortnite*. Most online multiplayer games have a number of different levels for players to explore. *Fortnite* only has one level. But that doesn't mean there isn't plenty to see and do. *Fortnite*'s world is made up of a giant island. It takes a long time to see the whole thing and learn all of its secrets!

Climb the stairs of an old house and you might stumble across a strange scene like this.

Plenty to See

There is a lot of variety on the *Fortnite* island. You can find snowy mountains and sandy beaches. You can battle other players in city streets or forest campgrounds. There are cool hidden areas to discover. There are even plenty of funny details to find tucked away.

An Ever-Changing World

Tired of the scenery on the island? Don't worry. It never stays the same for long. *Fortnite*'s **developers** are always making changes and adding new things to see!

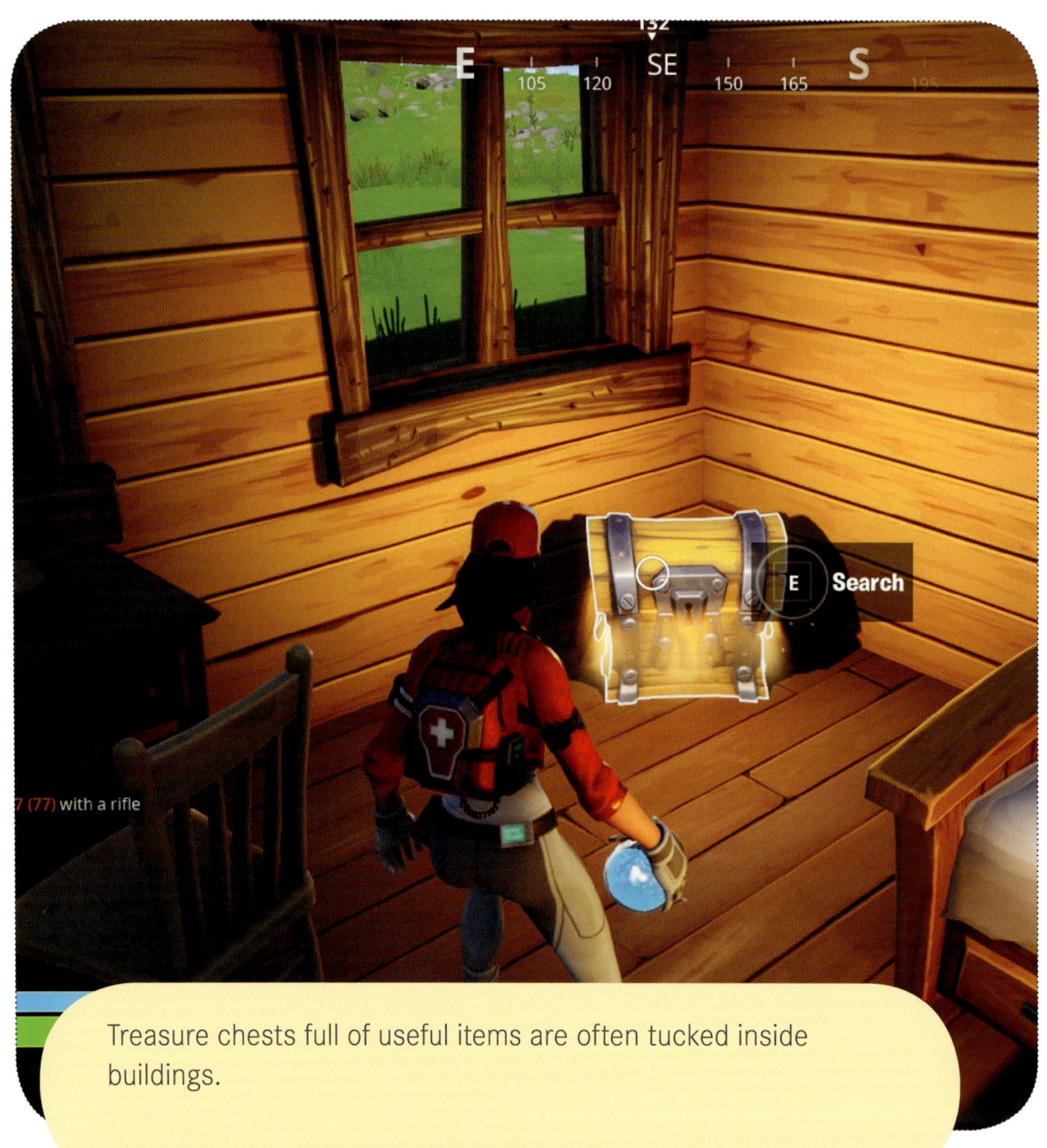

Treasure chests full of useful items are often tucked inside buildings.

Learning Your Way Around

Top *Fortnite* players learn everything they can about the island. It is easier to win if you know your way around. You will know where you can **scavenge** the best items. You will also know where other players are likely to gather. This helps you plan your attacks more carefully. Try to explore every corner of the island!

Try to learn the best ways to travel from one area to another on the island.

Checking the Map

Your in-game map will help you learn your way around. You can open it at any time while you are playing. You can even open it while you are still on the Battle Bus. Click anywhere on the map to drop a pin. This will put a colored light above your chosen location. You can see it even after you close the map.

The number by the glowing colored pin tells you how far away the pin is.

Deciding Where to Drop

You get to choose your starting location at the beginning of every match. You can jump from the flying Battle Bus anytime. Then you can skydive to the place you want to go. Look at your map before you jump. Drop a pin on the place you want to visit. Then glide toward it. Teammates can see your pin, too. You can all head toward the same spot.

If you spot something that stands out from the landscape, it is probably a landmark. Be sure to investigate!

Filling in the Blanks

Your map is completely gray when you first start playing *Fortnite*. The only way to color it in is to visit all the areas of the island. Some areas are major locations. At first, they are shown as question marks on your map. After you visit them the first time, your map will show their names instead.

Leveling Up

You will earn XP when you visit a new area of the island for the first time. XP are points that help you level up and unlock new **skins** and other items in *Fortnite*. This means exploring is really worth your time!

You are likely to run into other players in popular areas such as Sweaty Sands.

Seeking Out Supplies

The first thing to do after landing is find useful supplies. There are weapons, healing items, and building **materials** everywhere. The best places to look are usually inside buildings. Head toward one of the named major locations on your map. These places usually have a lot of buildings. This means they also have a lot of items!

Boats have built-in weapons so you can fight back if you are attacked while driving.

A Faster Way to Travel

Do you wish you could move around the island faster? Look for a vehicle. Different vehicles are available at different times. For example, the Chapter 2 update added boats to the game. Boats are one of the fastest ways to get around. There are all kinds of waterways crisscrossing the island. They are almost like highways for boats!

This barn could be a good hiding spot to launch a surprise attack. Or you could knock it down to get building materials. It's up to you!

Gaining an Advantage

Look for features on the island that will give you an advantage over other players. High points let you attack enemies from above. Areas with lots of obstacles help you avoid attacks from far away. Think about your surroundings as you move around the island. Never stop exploring, and have fun!

Change the World

Is there something you'd like to change about the island? A building in your way? A mountain too steep to climb? Remember that you can destroy almost anything you see. Then you can build something new!

Glossary

developers (dih-VEL-uh-purz) people who make video games or other computer programs

materials (muh-TEER-ee-uhls) supplies needed to build something

scavenge (SKAV-enj) search for useful items

skins (SKINZ) different appearances for characters in *Fortnite*

Find Out More

Books

Cunningham, Kevin. *Video Game Designer*. Ann Arbor, MI: Cherry Lake Publishing, 2016.

Powell, Marie. *Asking Questions About Video Games*. Ann Arbor, MI: Cherry Lake Publishing, 2016.

Web Sites

Epic Games—Fortnite
www.epicgames.com/fortnite/en-US/home
Check out the official *Fortnite* website.

Fortnite Wiki
https://fortnite.gamepedia.com/Fortnite_Wiki
This fan-made website offers up-to-date information on the latest additions to *Fortnite*.

Index

Battle Bus, 11, 13
boats, 19
building materials, 17
buildings, 17, 21

Chapter 2, 19

developers, 7

exploration, 9, 15

healing items, 17
high points, 21

map, 11, 13, 15

named locations, 15, 17

obstacles, 21

pins, 11, 13

scavenging, 9, 17
skydiving, 13

teammates, 13

updates, 7, 19

vehicles, 19

weapons, 17

XP, 15

About the Author

Josh Gregory is the author of more than 150 books for kids. He has written about everything from animals to technology to history. A graduate of the University of Missouri–Columbia, he currently lives in Chicago, Illinois.

DISCARD/SOLD
FRIENDS MLS